T0072391

A Little Pot of Oil

A Little Pot of Oil

LIFECHANGE BOOKS

JILL BRISCOE

MULTNOMAH
BOOKS

A LITTLE POT OF OIL

Published in association with the literary agency of Alive Communications, Inc.
7680 Goddard Street, Suite 200, Colorado Springs, CO 80920

© 2003 by Jill Briscoe
International Standard Book Number: 978-0-7352-9155-3

Cover image by Steve Gardner, PixelWorks

Unless otherwise indicated, Scripture quotations are from:
The Holy Bible, New International Version
© 1973, 1984 by International Bible Society,
used by permission of Zondervan Publishing House
Other Scripture quotations are from:
The Holy Bible, King James Version (KJV)

Published in the United States by Multnomah, an imprint of the
Crown Publishing Group, a division of Penguin Random House LLC.

MULTNOMAH® and its mountain colophon are registered
trademarks of Penguin Random House LLC.

The Library of Congress has cataloged the hardcover edition as follows:
    Briscoe, Jill.
      A little pot of oil / by Jill Briscoe.
            p. cm.
        ISBN 1-59052-234-6 (hardcover)
        1. Christian life. 2. Holy Spirit. I. Title.
      BV4501.3.B753 2003
      248.4—dc21

                                                    2003009929

147028534

Table of Contents

HOPE FOR WHEN YOU'RE RUNNING LOW

You know the feeling—that awful sinking realization that you are running on empty. Out of gas. Out of steam. Out of options and ideas.

Maybe you know what it is to run out of food or shelter or money. Your cupboard is bare—or you don't even have a cupboard—and you don't have a clue where to turn next. Maybe you've been out of a job, and the fear of what *might* happen has drained you of your hope and energy. Or maybe you have plenty of money but have run out of meaning in your life (you can have plenty of material goods and still be empty).

Have you ever run out of relationships? It happens, and it's a miserable, lonely experience. Maybe there's a shortage of real friends in your life. Maybe your marriage has failed or your children are estranged or you've lost the ones you love to death.

Perhaps your emptiness is on the inside. You've run out of patience, understanding, endurance… or faith, hope, love, joy.

Or perhaps your emptiness is on the inside. You've run out of patience, understanding, endurance…or faith, hope, love, joy. Around the corner of your yesterday is a dream shattered, a fortune lost, a nasty lawsuit, a disastrous move—or a series of such unexpected losses—and now you can't muster the strength or courage to look around the corner to tomorrow.

You may have run out of health. You've tried the

last remedy you know, and it didn't work. You may have run out of independence or the time to put wrong things right. Or perhaps you're to the point that you realize you've run out of years to do what you always wanted to do.

One birthday my husband woke up and contemplated the cheerful cards waiting for him. Aware, as he has so often put it, that he has considerably more history than future, he commented wryly, "How can someone as old as me be as young as this?" He's certainly not the only one to feel that way.

All of us, no matter what age we are, know what it feels like to run out of something or someone at some time for some reason. But there is one thing you never need to run out of, and that is God. This reality is the very heart of this book. And I hope you will take it to heart, because it makes all the difference between running on empty and living a full, fulfilled life.

You see, God has promised to be with us forever, and forever is a long, long time. Even better, God has promised to live *within* us—not only filling us when we run low, but also filling us with so much love, so much power, and so much strength that we can pour ourselves out in love and service to others.

Does this mean God's people never get discouraged, never run out of kindness and patience and joy? There is a notion afoot that people who really know God will never run low, never mind actually run out of anything. But you only have to look in the Bible to see that that isn't true. Consider:

- Adam ran out of clothing, and Abel ran out of breath.
- Methuselah ran out of birthday candles, and Enoch ran out of time.
- Abraham ran out of courage, and Hagar ran out of hope.
- Moses ran out of patience, and Joshua ran out of battles.
- Caleb ran out of mountains, and Gideon ran out of sight.
- Ruth ran out of heathenism, and David ran out of self-control.
- Solomon ran out of wisdom, and Elijah ran out of steam.

- A widow ran out of food, and Nehemiah ran out of workers.
- Esther ran out of options, and Job ran out of friends.
- Israel ran out of songs, and Jeremiah ran out of parchment.
- Jonah ran out of the will of God, but then the whale ran out of supper!
- Zechariah ran out of words, and Joseph ran out of Bethlehem.
- John the Baptist ran out of mercy, and a man ran out of demons.
- A woman ran out of water, and a multitude ran out of bread.
- A young man ran out of clothes, and some soldiers ran out of a body.
- Paul ran out of Christians to persecute, and Peter ran out of faith.
- A couple ran out of truthfulness, and a church ran out of its first love.

The truth is that we all live in a fallen world, which means even God's people will run low on resources from time to time. Sometimes we'll run so low it feels like we're completely out. Even believers know how it feels to be running on empty.

But there's an important difference: God has given His people what we need to fill up when we run low. It's the incredible gift of Himself, dwelling inside us. It's the person of God we call the Holy Spirit. Or, as they used to call Him when I was a girl growing up in England, the Holy Ghost.

Chapter 1

THE HOLY WHO?

GETTING TO KNOW THE ONE
WHO FILLS OUR EMPTINESS

When I was six years of age, the Second World War was in full swing, and bombs were part of my life. We lived in Liverpool, which was not a good idea! The Liverpool docks were pounded night after night, and I seldom slept in my little pink bedroom. We would wait till the siren began and hurry down to the shelter our dad had dug for us at the end of our garden. When the horrible noises of death and destruction began, I would try to remember the prayers we had said in school that day. I usually couldn't concentrate long enough to remember them, though, because I was so distracted waiting for the next bang.

Every day in school, when it was time for prayers, we British schoolgirls stood demurely in orderly rows, with our heads suitably bowed and hands together, looking at our shoes. Prayers and Scripture readings were daily events in every English public school back then. I am thankful there was no separation of church and state, because my family did not attend church. Wherever would a British schoolgirl like me have heard of Jesus if not in "assembly" every morning at school?

I listened daily to our headmistress intoning the Apostles' Creed. We were supposed to say it with her, and by now I was proud to know some of it by heart. One particularly bad night, when the blitz just wouldn't quit, I tried frantically to recall the words I thought I knew.

"I believe in God the Father Almighty, Maker of heaven and earth." Well, I remembered that bit. I paused to wonder what God the Father, Maker of heaven and earth, thought about the carnage we humans were inflicting on His handiwork. *Not much,* I thought grimly.

Now, then, I mused, *what comes next? Oh yes.* "And in Jesus Christ His only Son our Lord…born of the Virgin Mary." What that was all about? I hadn't a clue. I forced myself to think of the words while I put my hands over my ears to shut out the horrible wailing of the bombs flying overhead.

"I believe in the Holy Ghost…" Suddenly my mind focused on those words: *the Holy Ghost.* And just who *was* the Holy Ghost? The words sounded strange to me, and a little scary. Did I believe in the Holy Ghost? Did my sister and all the other girls? No one had ever explained these mysterious words to me, so I didn't have any idea how the Holy Ghost could help a frightened child waiting to be buried by a bomb in an underground dugout in Liverpool.

It took me nine more years to find out the truth: that the Holy Ghost was the Comforter, the "one called alongside to help," the Advocate, who was actually aware of my plight and was praying for me. That He was someone who could hold me together inside and hush my fears to sleep—God Himself, able to fill the empty places in my life, to fill me up when I was running on empty.

The war was over by the time I knew that. England and our family had begun to rebuild our shattered lives. I was eighteen years old and at college, struggling to make sense of the little I believed. I had tried to figure out life and death on my own as best I could, but had run out of answers. So I tried to forget all about such deep questions; I rationalized my sin and called it "growing up."

Life at college was good, and I threw myself into the adventure—especially the fun. I had the privilege of attending a teacher-training institution in Cambridge, where there was no lack of ideas floating around as to the meaning of life. But the people I talked to in the quaint little tea shops and in the beautiful halls of learning seemed as confused as I was about what was really true. Self-sufficiency seemed to be the way to go—except deep inside I knew I was anything but self-sufficient. In fact, I was rapidly running out of the ability to be my own god and answer my own prayers. I had an enormous hole inside me that nothing seemed to fill.

Then I found Christ during a stay in hospital, and in a heartbeat everything changed. The emptiness in my life was filled with indescribable beauty and hope. In the words of a hymn:

> Heav'n above is softer blue;
>   Earth around is sweeter green!
> Something lives in every hue
>   Christless eyes have never seen;
> Birds with gladder songs o'erflow,
>   Flowers with deeper beauties shine,
> Since I know, as now I know,
>   I am His, and He is mine.
>
> *George Wade Robinson*

"Christless eyes"—that's exactly what I looked at life with before. But now, like the man healed by Jesus, I could testify: "I was blind but now I see." (John 9:25). I saw the truth about Jesus and about myself and the world, and that truth filled my heart and my soul. I also realized I had survived the war not to live for myself, but to live for Him who had saved me from death by bombs and death by sin.

Because at this point I had never darkened the door of a church, all of this was brand new to me. The Word of God was certainly an unknown treasure chest. I bought a Bible and opened its stiff covers. Wonderingly I began to ask questions of the text. I asked questions of other Christians as well. I had to. I was so biblically ignorant I didn't know if an apostle was the wife of an epistle! Who had translated the Scriptures, I wondered, and were they complete and accurate? What did the Bible claim about itself? What was a missionary?

Then gradually I came back full circle to my question in the bomb shelter that awful night nearly ten years before: Who was the Holy Ghost? The words still conjured up a sheet-shrouded

> *Who had translated the Scriptures, I wondered, and were they complete and accurate? What did the Bible claim about itself?*

spook that haunted old English graveyards. But there they were in my Bible, so they must be important.

I learned from the sweet girl who had led me to the Lord that the Holy Ghost had nothing to do with graveyards and in fact had more to do with life than death. The Holy Ghost—or the Holy Spirit—was a person, not a thing, and He was deity. He was an equal member of the Trinity—as much God as my heavenly Father and Jesus Christ were. And He was an entity I could receive into my life. In fact, I had *already* received Him. The Holy Spirit had come to abide in my heart when I asked Christ to forgive my sin and invade my life.

I remembered doing that, of course. It had been almost ridiculously simple: "Come into my heart, Lord Jesus," I had prayed. Now I was assured that when I invited Him, He had indeed come by His Spirit. As the weeks unfolded, I became more and more aware that He had silently taken up residence in my soul. And I was soon to learn much more about how the Spirit worked.

As I began to read the New Testament, for example,

I found I was being mysteriously helped. Someone was throwing light on the words on those thin pages between the stiff covers of my King James Bible, enabling me to understand the Word of God. Of course, I soon came across these words of Jesus: "When he, the Spirit of truth, is come, he will guide you into all truth" (John 16:13, KJV). And "[The Spirit] shall take of mine, and shall shew it unto you" (v. 15, KJV).

So I came to understand that the Holy Ghost was my teacher. I read the Bible, and He interpreted what I was reading and applied it to my life. I couldn't get enough. My wondering heart was eager with expectation as the gospel became a reality to me.

I remember weeping as I tried to grasp the incredible story—how the Father had walked down the stairway of heaven with a baby in His arms and laid Him in a bale of hay—God's own essence in human form, here to turn this tired world upside down. Born of a woman Christ came, as Charles Wesley so beautifully put it:

Our God contracted to a span,
    Incomprehensibly made man.

I had no trouble believing that Christ had lived a perfect life. Of course. Why not? He was God! In a body like ours He walked our roads, ate our food, slept in our beds, and experienced our joys and sorrows. He taught us, loved us, rebuked us, and comforted us. He showed us how to know God, love God, and serve God. And to equip and enable us for this amazing calling, He sent the Holy Spirit into the world to fill us up when we start to run low on faith or hope or love, to make it possible for us to follow Him.

ALL OF GOD IN ALL OF ME

The night I was saved, the girl who led me to Christ told me to go to sleep saying, "All of God in all of me." I took her advice and so have never had a problem with the realization that when I received Christ by His Spirit, I received *all* of Christ *by* His Spirit. If the Spirit is a person, then you can't receive a "bit" of the Spirit, just as you can't receive only part of a person. So I had been given all of God I was going to get. My job from then on was to make sure He was receiving all of me. I needed to learn all I could about this Holy Guest and to cooperate with Him in His saving, satisfying, and sanctifying work in my life. As I kept in step with the Spirit and tried not to grieve Him, quench Him, resist Him, or insult Him, I would not only run on full instead of on empty, but I would also be able to pour out that fullness into the lives of others.

In the years following, I have never stopped learning about the Spirit's sweet, abiding presence. He has drawn me to Christ as Savior and Lord and has ignited a passion in my soul for those who do not know Him. He has taught me how to pray when I didn't have a clue what to say, enlightened my mind to the Scriptures and thoroughly applied them to my life, and overwhelmed me with grace. He has strengthened me when I was weak, humbled me when I was proud, and sensitized me to sin. In fact, He has been all that I have needed Him to be, whenever I have needed Him.

I am so glad the girl who first introduced me to Christ took time to explain that although I really did receive all of God—including the Holy Spirit—when I accepted Christ as Savior, there would *still* be times when I would grieve the Spirit and when I would run out of the will to be faithful, to be vocal about my faith, or to be holy. When life would deal me a hard hand or my friends would let me down, when a loved one would hurt me or I would simply run out of steam, sometimes my reaction would be anything but what would make the Lord's heart smile.

When that happened, she said, what I needed to do was pray. And so I learned that prayer isn't something you do; it's somewhere you go. When you run out of something important, you go to God. So if I ran out of holiness, I needed to run to the holy One, who would restore and forgive me.

That's a vital word for anyone who is running low or running on empty. Whatever it is you are running out of, let me urge you to run to God. If you run out of faith and hope and courage, you can run to Him for strength and inspiration. If you run out of marriage and your spouse runs out on you, you can go to God, who never runs out on anybody. If you run out of holiness and feel shopworn and

Prayer isn't something you do; it's somewhere you go.

grubby inside, you can run to God, who never runs out of mercy. If you run out of steam when you are going full tilt in life or ministry, you can run to God, who wants to fill you up again. The Word of God teaches us about staying in touch with the fullness of God through prayer, so we need never be empty.

You can also go to the Bible for both instruction and comfort. I learned that in the days after my conversion. The Holy Spirit was showing me so much, and I couldn't put that holy book down. While at college, I would sneak away at lecture breaks and get on my knees in front of that book and read passages, seeing images and pictures that were contemporaneously relevant to me and to my Cambridge world of cynics and skeptics and rank unbelievers. It was as if the Father had picked me up, put me on His knees, and opened a picture book that He had taken endless trouble to put together just for me.

I felt bad that I had lived all my life in England, where there were churches on every corner, yet was so ignorant of biblical doctrine. Why had I not investigated the Christian faith before? I was encouraged to discover, however, that I was not alone in my ignorance about the doctrines of the Bible, especially of the Holy Spirit. I read in the Acts of the Apostles that the disciples were confused about Him, too.

WAITING FOR THE WIND

The dark days after Jesus' crucifixion left His disciples in total confusion. Terrified, they huddled in secret behind locked doors. When would the authorities come, they wondered, and take them away to be crucified as well? They had run out of dreams, out of plans, and out of the courage to stand up for Christ in a world gone mad. Now that He was dead, they had certainly run out of the belief that they had the power to follow the Master's ideals and teachings. They were truly running on empty.

But then Christ rose from the dead, and the disciples heard about a dead man walking. Witnesses insisted the man who had risen from the dead was Jesus. The disciples began to remember things He had told them—including His promise that He would rise from the dead on the third day. Still they hardly dared to believe it—until Jesus showed Himself alive with "many infallible proofs" (Acts 1:3, KJV). He appeared to individuals among their company and then showed Himself to them all at one time. It was true! Though the doors stayed locked, He was there.

So they believed—how could they not? But still they found themselves weak, frightened, and unsure what to do, especially after Christ had ascended and they were left to carry on without Him. Though Jesus had promised to send them a "Helper," promised to pour out His "Spirit" upon them, they had no idea what that could mean.

Until Pentecost, that is.

I had heard about Pentecost growing up. Our school had even enjoyed a holiday on the day. But the Pentecost events I read about in the Acts of the Apostles were far more amazing and important than any schoolgirl holiday.

A hundred and twenty disciples, both men and women, were all together in Jerusalem, in an upstairs room, waiting just as Jesus had told them to do. They didn't know it then, but they were doing what we all need to do when we're running low on our own strength. They were waiting to be filled with the Holy Spirit. They were waiting for the wind.

And then it happened, just as the Lord Jesus had promised. Those who heard it said it sounded like a mighty storm approaching—like a rushing wind. It brought people running out into the streets of Jerusalem to find out what the noise was all about. The power of God had come pouring in to be what the disciples couldn't be and do what they couldn't do, to tell what they feared to tell and take them where they feared to go. God came calling that day. He came to stay, in the form of the indwelling Holy Spirit. And ever since, He's been the answer to all our running-on-empty dilemmas.

HOPE FOR A RUNNING-ON-EMPTY WORLD

I have lived fifty years now since the Holy Spirit came into my heart. It's been nearly two thousand years since He came at Pentecost. And yet so much of our world still seems to be running on empty—waiting for the wind.

As in the days of Pentecost, half the world has never yet heard of Jesus, and the half that has heard often seems powerless to take the message out into the increasingly hostile streets of Jerusalem, Judea, and the uttermost parts of the earth. Meanwhile, it seems, the world is running out of time. It is fast running out of hope. It is running out of land, food, and water; forests and medicine. It is running out of natural resources, cash, and goods. It is running out of shelter and the basic necessities of life.

Today, in our frightening new millennium, people's hearts are failing them for fear. Who of us doesn't wonder if our world is running out of peace? People in high places certainly seem to be running out of solutions to an ever-present security crisis. Even in the wealthy suburbs, wicked people climb in through the windows and steal and murder and rape children. In the privileged parts of the world, where you will read a book like this, people are running out of mean-ingful relationships. Love is in short supply. Nothing seems to last. Folks are running out of purpose and meaning. Many people are depressed, overeating, and desperately searching for comfort and intimacy. And even those in the church are running out of energy and ideas about how to fulfill the great commission and reach our generation with the gospel.

Nearly two thousand years after Pentecost, the world is still waiting for the wind.

Surely it is time for a personal Pentecost in all our lives, time for the breath of God to come and bring life into deadness, joy into sorrow, peace into pain, power into weakness. Now more than ever, we need the healing fullness of the Holy Spirit in our lives and in our running-on-empty world. This was brought home to me one fateful day in September of 2001.

I was in the air on September 11, trying to get back to Chicago from Europe. All I heard from my fellow passengers that day was "I want to go home." This was quite understandable, because all 250 of us were stranded in Newfoundland with nowhere to go.

Surely it is time for a personal Pentecost in all our lives.

We were on United Flight 929, high in the sky over the Atlantic Ocean, when the two airplanes hit the World Trade Center towers. Our captain dumped fuel into the ocean and made a swift but sure emergency landing in Canada. As we peered out of the airplane windows, we saw we were not alone. Well over fifty planes from Europe were lined up tidily on the runways, waiting to be processed. At that point we still didn't know what had happened, but we would soon find out. The world had changed while we were in the air.

Our planeload settled in for what turned out to be twelve hours on the runway and six days on friendly Salvation Army pews in Gambo, Newfoundland. *What did it all mean?* we wondered, as everyone's hearts turned toward home.

"I want to go home," said the beautiful young woman in the coffee queue next to me one morning at breakfast. She voiced her longing almost to herself. I assumed she must have a loving family worried sick about her. But I soon found out that wasn't the case. Her home, in fact, was really just an empty house. But that didn't matter to her. It didn't seem to matter to anyone. Even those people whose homes were dysfunctional or empty still wanted to go there.

I understood. I shared those feelings. But vying with that longing to go home and have my mother put her arms around me and "kiss it better" (even though she had been dead for years) was another emotion—a certain strange acceptance of the situation. When I examined the emotion, I understood what it was: contentment with my circumstances and an underlying excitement and anticipation that these were going to be six of the most God-shadowed days of my life. The Spirit I knew so well by now was still dwelling in me, filling me up even in the most fearful of circumstances.

"I just want to go home," the beautiful woman said again.

I took a deep breath and said quietly, "I *am* home."

She looked up, startled.

"Home is the will of God," I continued. "I happen to believe that for those who love the Lord, nothing can happen that He doesn't allow."

She gazed at me. "Explain that to me."

So I told her about the first thing that had popped

into my mind as I tried to absorb the pilot's announcement that there had been a national emergency, that all the airspace and borders in America were closed, but that he couldn't tell us why till we were on the ground. I immediately thought of a verse from the Bible, Psalm 139:16: "All the days ordained for me were written in your book before one of them came to be." That meant every day—even September 11, 2001.

I then told her my story and explained that when the Holy Spirit comes to make His home in us, He makes us feel at home in the will of God. That's one of the reasons He abides in our lives. I took time to explain Pentecost to her, and I tried to impress upon her the wonder of the indwelling Christ, who fills up our emptiness.

I also talked to this young woman about the Scriptures and explained that the Bible is a collection of writings penned across thousands of years in many different styles and genres. "It is also a storybook," I explained. "God inspired the biblical writers to take a variety of approaches so all of us can find at least one style that clicks."

"I am a visual learner," my new friend offered.

"Then you'll be intrigued with the pictures and symbols of Scripture," I said. This gave me a marvelous opportunity to use some of the stories and symbols from the Bible to explain to her the gospel—the only thing that holds the answers for our weary, worn-out, running-on-empty world.

Chapter 2

POURED OUT
AND FILLED UP

THE STORY OF THE LITTLE POT OF OIL

The symbols in the Bible have always intrigued me. More important, they have lit up the most difficult passages and shed light on complicated concepts. When God wanted to tell us about the Holy Spirit, who is part of the Godhead—for God is three persons in one—He used straight talk, but He also used pictures and symbols to help us to understand the reality behind them. Among the symbols used in the Bible to describe the Holy Spirit are the gentle dove of peace, the fire that ignites, a wind that is mysterious but has visible effect—remember the Pentecost story?—and water that refreshes and flows from our lives.

Yet another important symbol for the Holy Spirit's work in our lives is that of oil. Both now and in biblical times, oil is an important substance. It nourishes. It lubricates, making things work better. It provides energy to our bodies and can be burned to provide light. It binds and soothes and unites. In the Bible, people or objects were anointed with oil for different reasons. Special oil was created for medicinal, preservative, and cosmetic objectives. It was also used for burning in lamps. God invested anointing oil with religious significance, too. Prophets, priests, and kings were anointed with holy oil when they were set apart to serve God.

So what does the symbol of oil tell us about the Holy Spirit? It speaks to us of, among other things, God's ability to help us live the life He calls us to. And it tells something about how He works in us.

So often people have said to me, "I am afraid I will let the Lord down. I can't be good enough or kind enough, clever enough or patient enough or unselfish enough." In fact, I have known people to not respond to an invitation to accept the Lord for this very reason. But He is our Helper, the one who makes it possible for us sinful humans to follow Jesus. He is love, joy, patience, and peace even when we are hateful, impatient, joyless, and confused. When life brings us low for whatever reason, He can empower us to stand up straight and keep on keeping on. When we run out of power to be and to do what we ought, the Lord has only just begun to supply us with His strength to live well beyond what we can do on our own.

When life brings us low for whatever reason, He can empower us to stand up straight and keep on keeping on.

There is an incident in the book of 2 Kings (4:1–7) that illustrates what I am talking about. It is a true story and a symbolic lesson, too—about a widow, the prophet Elisha, and a little pot of oil. Let me tell you the widow's story. Maybe you'll find that you can relate, even if you are not a widow. I have returned to the lessons of this story over and over again, especially when I seem to have "run out" of the will to "run on."

A WIDOW'S WORRY

The widow lady in this story was truly running on empty. She had run out of a whole lot of things. First, she had run out of marriage; her husband had died. And she was not only a widow, but a young widow. We know she was young because she had young children. There's no doubt that life had dealt her a cruel blow.

I was speaking at a widows group one day, and a new member of the group, a woman in her thirties, was trying to describe how she was feeling. "I feel like half a pair of scissors," she explained. "I am experiencing an intimate loneliness that perhaps only someone who has been happily married and then cruelly bereaved knows. And yet at this moment, I do not feel anything at all. I am numb." There were no tears, just a terrible, dry despair. She had not only run out of a husband; she had run out of emotions, too.

On the other hand, I have spoken to some who have been deprived of a loved one through death or divorce and who are in so much emotional pain they can hardly breathe. Unlike the woman I met in this group for widows, they cannot stop weeping. And they believe they have nothing left to live for. When you are experiencing one long scream on the inside, God hears the cry of your broken heart. He counts your tears. He truly feels your pain. When you have lost someone you love, God really does come calling.

In the meantime, listen to what happened to the widow in the story in 2 Kings. Not only was her heart broken because she had lost her husband; she had also run out of money. She no longer had the means to support herself and her family.

When you are experiencing one long scream on the inside, God hears the cry of your broken heart.

This woman and her husband, you see, had belonged to one of the schools of the prophets that Elisha's mentor, Elijah, had set up. They were groups of prophets in training. Now that her husband was gone, however, she had no way to pay her husband's creditors. This was serious for her because it meant she had not only run out of cash, but she might also lose her children. She could well be facing the loss of her two precious boys. It worked like this.

God had instructed the leaders of Israel to make careful provision for the widows who lived among them. One of the ways they did this was by allowing creditors to take a widow's dependent children and put them to work in the employ of a fellow Israelite. Here they could be provided for and also learn a skill or trade. In the next sabbatical (or seventh) year, when according to Jewish law debts were forgiven, the children could return to their extended family. However, the sabbatical years had not always meant freedom for children who had been taken by creditors as collateral. Many times the children were prevented from returning to their mothers and providing for them because of the selfishness of their masters.

This was the widow's great fear. If the creditor took her children, she might never get them back again. As she told Elisha, she feared they would end up as slaves.

Many of you reading this book fully understand this widow's dilemma. You have experienced her worst fears. Perhaps you have stood in a divorce court and heard the judge declare that your ex-spouse will have custody of the children. It has not been a creditor coming to your door, but your ex-spouse and his lawyers. Maybe you ran out of money to defend yourself. No wonder you've found yourself running on empty in a situation like this!

Or you may not be bereaved, but you may, like this little widow, be bankrupt. She went and complained to the prophet Elisha about her dilemma: "I have nothing in the house," she told him. Maybe you share her despair. For whatever reason, you feel you have "nothing in the house" either.

And like the widow, you may feel bitter and hurt and angry. "Your servant, my husband, is dead," was her pointed comment, "and you know that he feared the Lord." This is the voice of anger that has been held in till it can be held in no longer. Not only was this woman running out of the wherewithal to provide for her children; she was running out of the most important thing: faith in her God. And make no mistake about it—running out of things that are precious to us often leads to our running out of faith.

Once, as I visited with a woman, I noticed a picture of her grandchildren on the piano. "What beautiful children," I commented. "Do they live near you?" She nodded yes. "But I only get to see them once a year, and then only for two hours." I looked at her, speechless. "It is the divorce," she explained. "Our daughter-in-law got full custody, and she is in control. I find myself going to the grocery store in hopes they will be there, too. And I keep wondering where God can be in all this."

A grandmother of thirteen myself, I could only imagine that woman's pain. She had spent all her life thinking about the input she would have into her grandkids' lives. Now they were far away from her in every sense of the word, and her bereavement was beginning to undermine her trust in God.

Have you experienced such faith distress? What did you do? Did you go numb—or strike out in anger? Did you withdraw from your pain and go into hibernation? Did you try to forget your troubles and turn to drugs or drink? Maybe you just packed up and moved, tried to run away. If you did, it probably didn't help because you took your pain along with you.

THE COURAGE TO CRY OUT

To her credit, the desperate widow in the 2 Kings story didn't run away—although she might have wanted to. But she needed help desperately. One thing had led to another, and she found herself incapable of being the caregiver anymore. She was in need of care herself. Sometimes having to receive instead of give can bring us to the point of running on empty quicker than anything else. One who is accustomed to giving finds it almost impossible to receive care, even when she desperately needs it.

Since my husband stepped down from his position as senior pastor of Elmbrook Church in Milwaukee, Wisconsin, we have represented the church in a worldwide "at large" ministry. That means I fly a lot these days, and I hear a lot of those little spiels given by the flight attendants at the beginning of the journey. The instructions are so familiar that no one seems to take any notice. The other day, however, my attention was caught as I watched the flight attendant demonstrate the use of oxygen masks in an emergency.

"If you are traveling with a small child," she said, "secure your own mask first, then assist your child."

It had occurred to me before that those familiar instructions would be difficult for me to follow. In an emergency, my mothering instinct would push me to care for my child first. But there's obvious sense in those instructions: If I didn't care for myself, I would be *incapable* of caring for my child.

Surely there's a lesson there for those of us who are used to being in a nurturing or caregiving role—not just mothers, but as pastors, teachers, missionaries, or church members. How can we be effective in giving life to others when we are gasping for spiritual breath ourselves? We need to accept help for ourselves before we will be in a position to bring life to others. Yet we who are used to being the caregivers often find it hard to receive help. So we continue trying to help others until we, too, are running on empty.

I remember sitting in that Salvation Army hall in Newfoundland, wishing desperately for a change of clothes. We had been told to leave our luggage on the plane, so I had nothing to change into. To make things worse, I had been on my way home from six weeks in Russia and had not changed clothes for four days prior to the flight. So I sat there feeling sticky, dirty, and miserable.

Suddenly a Salvation Army officer appeared and made an announcement. There had been a donation of clean underwear, and those of us who wanted to receive some needed to get up and form a line.

Did I need what he was offering? Oh, yes.

Did I leap up to get in line? Oh, no!

You have no idea how hard it was for me to admit what I needed. I knew it was stupid to be embarrassed, but I was.

I thought of the days at the height of the Croatian-Serbian conflict, when I had been part of a delegation for World Relief. In my mind's eye I saw myself handing out clothes to the thousands of refugees who were flooding over the border into Croatia. Back then I had no problem at all announcing that there was clean underwear for everyone. So what was wrong with me now? Well, for people like me, it is a whole lot easier to be the caregiver than to be the one cared for.

The widow in the story, however, was driven well beyond pride or embarrassment. She had no problem asking for help. She was desperate to survive, desperate not to lose what was left of her family.

Fortunately, someone who could help her was within hearing distance. His name was Elisha. When the widow was running on empty—out of husband, out of funds, out of faith—this prophet was running on full.

It was not that Elisha was rich and the woman was poor. They were both poor in material goods. They lived an ascetic life in the company of the prophets, and none was wealthy as the world counts wealth. But Elisha was rich by God's measure. He knew the Giver of all good things, the Father of lights, who delights to hear his children's prayers and to give them the things that they need.

So here is another thing that is important to

remember: God is so good when we have run out of what we need. He delights to arrange to have someone around the corner of our dilemma who is running on full and can pour into our lives just when we need it most. But for that to happen, we have to cry out. We have to cast ourselves on God in the middle of the awful mess and see what He will do or whom He will send to help us, for God often does His work through ordinary people.

Look around you. Think of all the people you know. Who of these has a vibrant faith? Who is a woman or man of prayer? That person is your Elisha. That's who you need to turn to when you're running low.

It's not always easy to ask for help though, just as it isn't easy to accept the help that is offered. There are a thousand reasons we don't do it.

I well remember a time when I was running on empty. I was a young mother with three children under school age. My husband and I were serving a youth mission that required his being away for long periods of time. Life was serious and stretching for us in those days. I knew that God had called us to this work, yet I often felt tired, confused, worried, and overworked. I could certainly relate to the little widow who had lost her husband and was in danger of losing her children. Although my husband was alive and well, I felt like a ministry widow. How could I be both mom and dad to the kids so they wouldn't grow up to resent the Lord? I really did feel I was left with "nothing in the house."

The interesting thing was that I, too, had an Elisha just up the road. She was within walking distance. But I didn't walk the distance to talk to her—at least not at first. She was within phone distance, but I didn't dial her number. She was in prayer distance, but I didn't ask her to pray for me.

Don't be afraid to cry out when you run out.

Why? Pride, maybe. I didn't want anyone to know I couldn't be the bionic missionary wife I had thought I was. And I was ashamed of my neediness. All around me were women who also saw little of their husbands. They seemed to have everything under control, while there I was falling apart.

I can't believe I wasted so much time being miserable when the help I needed was so close. But I did. I couldn't bring myself to ask for help until I was absolutely desperate. But only when I finally cried out did things start getting better.

So don't be afraid to cry out when you run out. The Lord will come swiftly to your aid. He may send an earthly person like Elisha to help you, or He may supply you personally with what you need. But none of this is likely to happen until you swallow your pride or your shame or your fear and cry out. It all depends on your depending.

Remembering What You've Forgotten

As soon as I finally asked my Elisha for help, of course, I wished I had come sooner. And so, I am sure, did the little widow. After she cried out to him, Elisha's immediate response was "How can I help you?" But his approach to helping her was a little surprising. He didn't give her money, and he didn't help her with her accounting. Instead he asked, "What do you have in the house?"

"Nothing," she replied. That was the problem—she was running on empty, remember? But then she remembered that the cupboard wasn't completely bare. "Nothing," she corrected herself, "but a little pot of oil." In her extremity, she had forgotten all about that oil.

And that is what happens to all of us. We have within us all that we need in the person of the Holy Spirit, represented by the little pot of oil. But when trouble with a capital *T* comes calling, we forget our all-sufficient resource. We forget that He is here to give us the wisdom we lack, the words to speak, the actions to take. We forget that the Bible says we can draw on His comfort and rely on Him to fill us up when we run low. It is the Holy Spirit who garrisons our hearts with peace in the most impossible of circumstances. And

We have within us all that we need in the person of the Holy Spirit, represented by the little pot of oil.

because He is always there and available, we are never really running on empty.

It's funny how when you're at Wits' End Corner you can think you have nothing in the house, when in reality you have everything. You may have no family, no food, no clothes, no future, no spouse, no health, or no children, yet be rich beyond your wildest dreams because you have the Holy Spirit in your life.

The trick, then, is to remember the resources we have. That's what Elisha helped the widow do. Instead of simply giving her what she needed, he persisted in directing her toward where her help lay…until she finally remembered what she had forgotten.

The prophet could have used that widow's need as an opportunity to show his own wisdom and goodness. He could have gone out and collected donations or negotiated with the woman's creditors and then taken all the recognition for helping her. Instead, he turned her back to God. He asked her what she had and showed her how to draw on that resource.

Elisha told the woman what she needed to hear. Then he gave her something to do. And it was an amazing thing he told her to do, yet she did it.

The widow did what she was told. After all, she really had nothing to lose. And what she gained through her obedience was a miracle. First, she sent her sons out to collect jars from all the neighbors, just as Elisha had told her to do. She then began to pour the oil, and from that one little jar she filled container after container—until she had enough to sell and satisfy her debts.

Have you nothing to lose? Have you tried everything and nothing is working out?

Shut the door on the world and throw yourself on God. It is fine to cry out to a person for help—and God may well provide for you through other people. But even then, your primary source of sustenance still needs to be the Lord.

That's exactly what Elisha was trying to teach the widow. If he had invited himself into the widow's small house and worked the miracle for her, then no one would have been

Shut the door on the world and throw yourself on God.

surprised. After all, this was a mighty man of God; what would you expect? But this time, wisely, Elisha insisted the miracle be between the widow and God—so she could see how sufficient the Lord really was for her.

Maybe that's a lesson you need to learn, too. Have you ever felt that God would never listen to your prayers? Perhaps you have no problem whatsoever believing that God hears the prayers of bionic Christians, but you wonder why He should listen to you. Do you feel unworthy, lacking in the faith you need? Then you need the lesson of the widow who was running on empty. You need to learn it's not the *amount* of your faith, but the *object* of your faith, that makes the difference.

My husband and I live on a small fishing lake that freezes over during the Wisconsin winter. In the middle of winter, the ice is usually thick enough to walk on. But we always test the ice carefully before trusting ourselves to it because we've learned that the thickness of the ice is much more important than our faith in the ice. We can have very little faith in very thick ice and still stay dry and safe. Or we can have lots of faith in very thin ice and drown by faith. With ice, as with life, the object of your faith is what really matters.

Elisha wanted the widow to remember that they worshiped the very same God—the God who hears the cry of the widow and the orphan as much as He attends to the king and the prophet. Elisha wanted her to experience firsthand the all-sufficiency of God's provision, to remember that as long as God is present, our lives will never be truly empty.

At some point in our lives, we all need to "shut the door" and exercise personal faith in God, to trust directly in His provision. The faith of our parents will not help us. The faith of our pastor will not help us. We need to stop and ask what we have in our own house and realize that the little pot of oil already on our shelves is truly enough to supply our needs.

THE POURING-OUT PRINCIPLE

That's exactly what happened to me when I ran so low as a young missionary wife. As I have mentioned, I did have an Elisha nearby. Our senior missionary's wife was at hand, just as Elisha was available to the little widow in 2 Kings. It took me a while to swallow my pride and go talk to her, but I managed to in the end.

I well remember the day I spilled out my frustrations to that loving woman. I told her about Stuart's long absences, about my worries over the children, about my difficulties juggling the roles of missionary, wife, and mother. I know there was resentment in my voice as I talked about these things, just as there was in the widow's voice as she complained to Elisha about the unfairness of it all.

Then my mentor did for me exactly what Elisha did for the little widow. First she listened. And then she firmly directed my attention toward the little pot of oil. In my stress, I had forgotten my greatest resource. I had discounted the work of the Holy Spirit in my life.

"You have all that you need within you, Jill," my Elisha reminded me, "in the person of the Holy Spirit. You have heavenly help a heartbeat away."

"So how does it work?" I asked.

"It works as you begin to appropriate what you have," she replied.

"How?"

"Go home, shut the door, and spend time with the Lord," she responded. "Then begin to pour out whatever you have into the empty vessels of your neighbors."

Well, that wasn't really the answer I expected to hear. I was already depleted, and she was telling me to empty myself further? I felt like I had nothing, and she was telling me I had to give away what little I had?

But that's exactly what I *needed* to do. My friend and colleague understood one of the most fundamental principles of living in Christ—that we have to empty ourselves in order to be filled. It's one of those paradoxes Jesus liked to pose for us—the first will be last, those of us who lose our lives will find them…and we only truly begin to be filled as we pour ourselves out for others.

My Elisha knew, in other words, that the answer to my emptiness would come not in seeking fulfillment, but in losing my life in service. It would come as I ministered to people who were hurting a whole lot more than I was. I needed to put my little troubles aside and start attending to the bigger troubles in other people's lives. And as I began to do that, my life would begin to fill up again.

Well, I was desperate enough to do what she told me. I went home, shut the door, and got on my face before God. I asked Him to show me where to start pouring out.

Give me an idea, Lord, I prayed. He did. He had been waiting to hear me ask Him that.

Then I got up off my knees, called a babysitter for the evening, and took off on my own to the town center. I went to one of the trouble spots where teenagers liked to hang out and just started talking to kids. And as I started to connect with a few of those at-risk teens, I began in effect to pour out into some empty teenage lives.

I had thought I had nothing in the house. I certainly had nothing left in myself to give. But as I began to talk to these beautiful kids, I was able to draw on the limitless power of the Holy Spirit, and as I poured out, He poured in. It was one of the most incredible evenings of my life.

That night was just the beginning. Whenever I could, I showed up where teens hung out in our town.

I would talk to them, offer them practical help if I could, share Scripture with them. I brought them home and fed them meals. And the more I poured myself out into these "vessels," the more love and faith and hope there seemed to be in my life.

Even better, our children became part of the miracle, just like the widow's boys in the story in 2 Kings. Her sons helped collect the jars. They watched the oil begin to flow. They saw the vessels fill up one by one. And so it was with our children, David, Judy, and Peter. They helped me minister to the teens, and they saw the results. They hung around for the Bible studies and listened to the questions. They watched as boys and girls came off drugs. They saw girls who were pregnant out of wedlock choose to have their babies instead of aborting them because they had come to understand the preciousness of human life to the Lord. They saw the oil keep on flowing, and my miracle became their miracle, too.

One of my chief worries in those early, challenging days had been that our children would resent the Lord because of the demands of living in a missionary family.

But just the opposite happened once I learned the pouring-out principle. It is no surprise to me, in fact, that all of our children are in ministry today. Once you have been part of such a life-giving experience, you will never be the same again.

PREPARING TO POUR

Sometimes it takes a crisis in our lives to test our faith, to show us the limits of our own strength and the sufficiency of God's provision. But we don't learn that lesson if we just sit around and wait for God to take care of us. We have to step out and pour out, trusting that the Holy Spirit will fill us and give us what we need to continue.

That doesn't mean there's nothing we can do *before* a crisis comes. Although it's possible for even the most "filled-up" Christians to come up empty at times, it only makes sense that the more "filling" we do in ordinary times, the more we'll have to draw on when our resources drop low.

It goes without saying, for instance, that it all starts with accepting Christ as your Savior and allowing the

Holy Spirit into your life. That's where your little pot of oil comes from in the first place. In addition, you can prepare for crisis by getting to know the Bible and learning how to look for help in its pages. When we allow Him to, God pours Scripture into our lives so that we can pour it out to others when we need to.

The way to start is to buy a Bible and start reading a good piece of it every day. Try to spend time in prayer and stillness as well, getting used to the sound of God's voice. Talk with other Christians and try to learn how faith works.

Do whatever you can, in other words, to keep your heart and life full of God's power. But don't worry when you seem to be running low on resources. That's when the power of the Spirit already living in you will have a chance to shine.

When I was a very new Christian, I had to go into hospital for an operation. All went well until right before I was supposed to leave, when I discovered a hernia caused by the surgery. One minute I was dressing to go home; the next minute I was undressed again and back on the operating table. This delay was not on my agenda. Even as a young Christian, however, I had already learned the verse I would later quote to the young woman in Newfoundland: "All the days ordained for me were written in your book before one of them came to be" (Psalm 139:16). So I prayed that I would be alert to what God had in mind by keeping me there for this unexpected stay. Then, as I prayed about the situation, an idea formed.

"Do you ever have a church service in the ward, Sister?" I asked the nurse.

"No, dear," she replied. "Only in the chapel."

"Would you like to have one in the ward for all the people who can't go to the chapel?"

"Well, who would do it?" she asked.

"Me." She looked at me, amazed. Apparently I didn't fit her idea of the kind of person who would hold church services. I'm not sure I fit *my* idea either, but I was pretty sure that was what God wanted me to do.

"Well, I don't see why not," she finally said. "I'll arrange a wheelchair for you." So it was done. But after the arrangements were made, I lay in bed aghast at my cheek at even suggesting such a thing. I had never put a "talk" together before and had only given my testimony a couple of times. What would all the patients think? They wouldn't even have an option as to whether to listen—because they were all stuck in bed.

The damage had been done, however. The sister was already putting up notices in other wards to see if anyone else wanted to attend the service. I would have to follow through with my rash offer. So I began to devour the Bible. I read and read and read. I covered much of the New Testament in the four days I had before Sunday came. I also tried to order my thoughts into an outline or plan. But they wouldn't be ordered, and soon the dreaded day was upon me. The nurses helped me into the wheelchair, put me in place, then wheeled others into the ward.

I felt faint at that moment. Despite all my preparations, I was sure I had nothing in the house. "Who are you?" the devil asked me, and to me his voice seemed loud enough for all the ward to hear. "Who are you to think you have anything important to say?"

"Nobody," I replied truthfully. "But I know

Somebody they need to hear." As new as I was to the faith, I sensed that all these people were waiting for the wind. And I had no idea what God had in mind for me to say, but I knew that God knew. And the Spirit knows what God knows: "No one knows the thoughts of God except the Spirit of God" (1 Corinthians 2:11).

The same book (1:27–28, KJV) says that God delights to use the foolish things of the world to confound the wise and the weak things to confound the mighty. *That's good,* I thought when I read that verse. *I surely qualify.*

So there I was in my wheelchair, feeling foolish and weak and empty, but determined to follow through with what God had started. I took a deep breath and began to talk about the temptations of Jesus. I have no idea why I picked that subject, but it seemed a good idea at the time. And I can't remember how my talk went or even what I said. But what I do remember is that the words and ideas kept coming, and I had the sense that they were poured into me as I poured them out.

I finished up by asking anyone who wanted to

accept Jesus to raise her hand. A girl halfway down the ward, lying flat on her back, did so. I wheeled my wheelchair furiously to her side and then led her to the Lord. Her name was Audrey, and she had been waiting for the wind a long time. I can still see her tears and joy all intermingled as we laughed and cried together. I told her lots of things that day, especially about the Holy Spirit, who knows what we need to say when we need to say it.

In the years since then, it has happened in my life so many times. I would feel as empty as the widow's house in 2 Kings. But then I would remember my little pot of oil. I would start to pour out, and then what I needed to say would pour in. And all those empty vessels who were waiting around me would be filled.

We so often want the whole thing the other way around. We want God to pour in what we need *before* we start pouring out. We expect Him to pour in some courage before we take action. We expect Him to pour in the strength and inspiration before we obey Him. But it doesn't work that way. We first have to be obedient to the promptings of the Spirit—to the ideas He puts in our heads. And then, after obedience, the power comes.

The Lord says not "I will fill your mouth first, and then open it," but "Open your mouth wide, and I will fill it."

Chapter 3

THE POT OF ALL

SECRETS OF FILLED-UP LIVING

All down the years, the principles I have learned from the widow and her pot of oil have stood me in good stead. For thirty years, for example, I was a pastor's wife, and there is plenty of opportunity for running low on resources when you are a pastor's wife. You live with people's expectations—and often their criticism. You and your husband are constantly on call to minister to the needs of others, putting your own needs on hold. When you're a pastor's wife, you can easily run out of self-worth, friends, money, and energy. You can run out of patience, charity, and compassion. But you never run out of oil.

In thirty years of church ministry, I learned that lesson over and over. Even when I was depleted, I could always rely on the Holy Spirit to empower and strengthen me, to pour Himself into me whenever I was obedient in pouring myself out for others.

During these years I also began speaking and writing. I began traveling, too, responding to invitations from around the country and later, when the kids were grown, from around the world. When my husband and I changed our functions on the church staff and began representing our congregation worldwide, the traveling began in earnest—and I began learning more and more about how that little pot of oil really works.

There was a time, for instance, during the process of writing this book. Stuart and I had just returned from many weeks of ministry in Australia and New Zealand. My husband had taken off again almost immediately, and I had just a few short days at home before I was scheduled to fly out again. Having been away from the kids and grandkids for five weeks, I immediately got in the car and drove to Chicago for the day to catch up with our daughter and her family. I got home late that night, glad I had gone, but aware that I had only two days left to catch up on business and repack for ministry in Israel and Jordan.

The next days at the office were long, and I was aware that my time for regrouping and packing was dwindling fast. At last I finished with the work at hand. But just as I was gathering my things, the telephone on my desk rang. I have to admit that I hesitated to pick it up. I answered and heard the rather distraught voice of a man telling me that his mother was dying. The man was calling to see if Stuart could do the funeral.

I knew the man's mother well. Jenny had been our neighbor when we first came to the States, and her husband was one of the first people who came to Christ because of our ministry. His was also one of the first funerals at which my husband had officiated here.

Even after that, Jenny had kept in touch and diligently prayed and supported us over the years, even though she had moved a good forty miles away. She had talked about the Lord to everyone who would listen, especially in her last days in the nursing home. She loved Stuart and me and had watched our TV program faithfully for years after being confined to her home. Anyone else within her orbit had been forced to watch it, too.

I told Jenny's son that Stuart was out of town and put him in touch with another pastor. Then I hung up the phone, already feeling guilty. *I should go and see her,* I thought. Of course, all the reasons I *shouldn't* go see her sprang immediately to mind. Not only was I still jet-lagged from New Zealand, but I had only this evening left to turn around. The hospice where Jenny was staying was at least an hour's drive away. And she was already unconscious, so she wouldn't even know if I was there. Anyway, she had her family around her, and a pastor was on call. She really didn't need me.

But God's still, small voice wouldn't let me alone. I felt horrible as I began to walk toward my car, ready to call it a day and head home.

The battle began. *Lord,* I prayed, *You know I'm exhausted. No one will know if I don't go to see Jenny except You and me. Anyway, I haven't even seen her for years and years.* But it was no good, because at once those three little words from 2 Kings 4 sprang to mind: "She kept pouring" (v. 5).

Then, Lord, give me the strength I need to make the trip, I prayed. I sat there waiting for the strength to arrive so I could head off up the freeway to see Jenny.

It didn't come. I still felt exhausted. But I also felt a little stirring of memory. I remembered the little pot of oil.

"Oh, Lord," I finally whispered. "After all these years, have I still not learned this lesson? Forgive me."

At once those three little words sprang to mind: "She kept pouring."

The Spirit was reminding me that I had to pour out *before* He would pour in. He would give me what I needed in order to do what He required, but first I had to obey the divine nudge. I had to set off in the direction of the need.

I sighed in pure weariness. Then, out of my nothingness, I obeyed. I put the car in gear, spun the wheel, and set off into the will of God for me that evening.

THAT'S HOW IT WORKS!

It took me forever to find the hospice. Then as I walked in the front door, Jenny's daughter saw me coming and burst into tears. But I didn't feel any better; in fact, I felt worse.

Going into Jenny's room, I found her unconscious and breathing heavily. The family hovered lovingly around the bed. I took Jenny's hand and began to talk to her. I thanked her for her sweet support and strong prayers down the years and for being a wonderful neighbor thirty-three years before, when we first arrived in this foreign land with our small family. I reminded her of her conversion and the conversion of her husband, Steve, as well. Then I told the crowd around the bed about Steve's funeral.

It had been my first American funeral, and I had been unprepared for many things, not least the open casket (we don't do it that way in England). Jenny stood by the bier and greeted the guests, and I stood beside her as her pastor's wife. The people kept coming. They would stop and pay their last respects, then pass on, relieved that their duty was done.

One grieving relative, however, took a long time in front of the casket. She kept saying over and over, "Oh, there he is, there he is. Just look at him—there he is!"

I must admit that I too was thinking, *There he is,* because the mortician had made Steve look better than I had ever seen him when he was alive. But Jenny had other ideas. She stood quietly as long as she could, and then she blurted out to the grieving relative, "No, no, you've got it all wrong—there he *isn't.* If I believed 'there he is,' I would not be able to shut that box and put him in the ground. Steve's not there in the casket. He's long gone to be with the Lord."

The woman looked at her in amazement. "Absent from the body," I interjected as Jenny warmed to her theme.

"Present with the Lord," she added.

The relative fled the room, and Jenny looked at me and smiled. "Let's tell everyone, Jill," she said. And so we stood there for hours, it seemed, while the new widow poured out her message of hope into the empty vessels of her neighbors.

"That's how it works, Lord, isn't it?" I breathed in

wonder. "We begin pouring out of our nothingness, and You pour in."

Jenny's hand moved in mine when I told that story in her hospice room. "She hears you," her daughter murmured. "The nurse said so." I felt confident she did hear me. Even though I couldn't see her face for the oxygen mask, I knew Jenny and I were savoring the memory together.

Who can know the joy of this but a poured-out Christian?

Driving back that evening, I got lost and arrived home late, still weary. But my heart was light as I contemplated the evening just past. How glad I was that I had gone to see Jenny. The Spirit had prompted me, empowered me, and spoken through me. Who can know the joy of this but a poured-out Christian who doesn't think she has anything in the pot to pour out?

WHAT'S MY JOB?

While we are here on earth, till we breathe our last, we will never run out of opportunities to pour out into the lives of others. In fact, pouring out to others is the reason we are here on earth in the first place. If we are believers, pouring out is our *job*—and the Spirit's filling is what makes it humanly possible.

I am more aware of this reality now than at any time in my life. Having stepped down from the pastorate after thirty years of service, Stuart and I at once stepped up to step out—and to minister, train, preach, and teach. In the two years since then, we have been on the road continually.

We relish this opportunity to "freelance for the Lord." And yet our fundamental job has not really changed—and it's not really any different from any other Christian's. Our job is still to pour out for others the love that has transformed our own lives. How we accomplish that job has changed a bit, though. And as Stuart and I roam the world as Elmbrook's Ministers at Large, I find myself on a continual learning curve.

I have been accustomed to speaking to large groups, for instance. But in some countries we visit, gathering together in large groups isn't wise or even possible, so Christians meet around a table for a meal, in a park, or just in twos and threes. Even where meetings are possible, they may well be very small. Most ministry happens casually, in informal encounters among Jesus lovers.

There is never any shortage in these places of lost people to share with or believers who need encouragement. I just have to do things a little differently than I am accustomed to. I am learning, for example, when to leave the pulpit behind me and simply talk of Jesus, as the Scripture says, when I "sit at home and…walk along the road" (Deuteronomy 6:7). The same passage tells me I can only do this if God's words are upon my heart (v. 6). So my job these days involves holding my heart in my hands before God and making sure that it is never empty—that it is filled with God's thoughts and ideas, His commands and promises, before I set out into the grand adventure of each and every day.

I've found that jet lag actually helps in this regard. I seem to be constantly awake while others sleep. And I used to toss and turn at such times and fret that I must sleep or I would be useless in the morning. But now I'm learning to use those late-night hours for being filled with God, knowing I will still be given the gift of strength when I need it. I use the time to fix my heart on the compass of God's will for me in the coming days of ministry. He and I talk about my phobias and fears, my uncertainties and inadequacies, and the incredible privilege of being in a strange place that needs Christ. Those sleepless hours have thus become an unexpected gift.

That doesn't mean I'm not tired. So often I'll find myself whispering, "I'm low, Lord. I'm all poured out." But then in the darkness He comes to me and He pours in. I don't necessarily feel it at the moment. But I certainly experience it the next day as I begin to collect all the empty vessels around me and start pouring. The Lord never disappoints me.

Prepared to Give an Answer

People often ask me, "What do you do on all these travels to faraway places?" I answer, "I just try to make sure I am available to God and to people on a moment-by-moment basis." That applies to what I do at home as well. In every part of my life, my job is to be ready to obey, ready to pour out.

First Peter puts it this way: "Always be prepared to

give an answer to everyone who asks you to give the reason for the hope that you have…with gentleness and respect" (3:15). Always means always—not just some days, not just Sundays. Not just when the jet lag is past, my stomach is back to rights, or my back isn't hurting. Not when I've had my sleep, taken a course of vitamins, or am feeling up and positive. My job is to be ready to be a blessing even when I could do with someone being a blessing to me.

The answer I am called to give may be to a grandchild as we fish on our little lake or to a thousand adults at a Sunday school convention. It could be a word to a neighbor who has lost a job or is being sued. I may even be called to be an Elisha to someone who is running on empty, gently turning his or her attention away from me and toward the replenishing power of the Holy Spirit in his or her life. And it may well be I have to do all this when I'm sick, counsel when I'm tired, and give a smile of encouragement when there is little to smile about.

And make no mistake, a smile can be a vital form of ministry. A genuine smile promises safety and invites conversation. It's yet another way of pouring out to others. But once again, the pouring comes from the Spirit within us. It is God Himself who makes our hearts smile with confidence and hope. The Holy Spirit scatters His love all over the place, starting inside a believer, and then we find the love of God spilling out into the world.

Your circumstances, of course, are different from mine. You may not travel or speak. You may not be involved in full-time ministry. And yet if you are a believer, your basic job description is the same as mine. It is to be full of the Holy Spirit and to pour yourself out to others in love and ministry, trusting in the Spirit to make that possible.

You need to be ready to give as you ask directions from a traffic cop or sit in a street-side café and converse with the waiter or give a coin to a beggar. You must be ready at the airport to smile at the people trying to keep us safe when a lot of people are frowning at the inconvenience—to say, "Thank you for doing a good job," and be rewarded with a shocked look and a grateful glance. (It's easy then to put a New Testament into their hands or invite a conversation.) God's vital work on any given day may well be done as you fill up the car with gas or show some interest in a child in the home where you visit. (I am old enough now to return to places we visited twenty or even thirty years ago and have young mothers tell me they still remember a story I told them at bedtime.)

I'm not saying that ministry to larger groups is not important. I would not have spent thirty years in a speaking ministry if I thought that. God calls some of us to minister through writing and speaking, and I believe we must honor that calling. And yet sometimes, in the middle of a heart-to-heart talk with a single parent or a rebellious missionary kid, a still, small voice will whisper inside me: "This is the reason you came thousands of miles." Or I may find some eternally important work that needs to be done with a woman (or two or three) who has never read any of the Bible, who in fact has never possessed one in her life and is hungry to know all about it. She could be a sophisticated young businesswoman in Jordan, an Indonesian shopkeeper, an Indian vendor, a teenage rocker in the former Soviet Union, or a supermarket clerk in my own hometown. I must be prepared to give an answer to any of these along the way, at any time, and in any place—but always in the power of the Spirit. That's my job, every day of the week.

CALLED TO COMPASSION

Part of my job, too, is to be filled with compassion for all peoples. And this is easier said than done. I know perfectly well that in Christ there is neither Jew nor Greek, black nor white, male nor female, bound nor free—that all are one in Christ Jesus. But the simple truth is that humanly speaking some people are a lot easier for me to get along with than others. Being English by birth and having lived in the United States for as long as I lived in England—in other words, having my feet planted firmly in the middle of the Atlantic—I find it isn't always easy to relate to the sometimes excitable Latins, the ultrapolite Japanese, the voluble Israelis, or the confrontational Russians. Plus, there will always be certain people I just don't hit it off with. But because I am a Christian, I don't have the option of only loving the people who make me comfortable. I have to do better than that.

For this I need Jesus. And fortunately, for this I *have* Jesus. Jesus wants me in people's lives, and what Jesus wants is far more important than what Jill wants. He loves them all. "Well, that's good," I mutter to myself, "but I need to love them, too." And the truth is that left to myself I only love those I am naturally drawn to.

The good news is that Jesus doesn't leave me to myself! In the person of the Holy Spirit, He pours the love of God into my heart. And I have discovered that there is always quite enough love to go around. As I pour out, sometimes in sheer obedience, giving love even to people I find difficult to like, He pours in the love of God that is deeper and wider than anything I could muster on my own. And that's important, because His kind of compassion often takes me places I would never choose to go. It's the kind of compassion that gets off the donkey and gets down and dirty in the ditch!

Here in the ditch there are no orderly rows of Christians assembled to listen to my Bible study, to greet the author and ask for an autograph, or to thank me for the impact I have had in their lives. Here in the ditch, the caliber of my character and spiritual maturity will be tested and seen. But here, too, the power of the Lord's love will be felt most deeply.

I will find a waiting world in my ditch. It may be a Russian woman who has had eight abortions in her lifetime or a little boy standing on one leg and looking at his world through one eye because he stepped on a land mine while herding his sheep. Or it might be the sullen teenager at the nearby playground or the woman down the street who is angry at the world because her husband left. There will doubtless be many who don't want me in their ditch at all and will rudely ask me to leave. Here in this dirty ditch, perhaps with no running water, are the lost people who have no idea they are lost because no one came to tell them. Here in this filthy place, I can take my oil and pour it into the deep wounds of the wounded men or women who surround me.

A DEPENDABLE SUPPLY

So what is my job? Once again, it's the same as your job. It is to step beyond the limitations of my own compassion in order to share Christ's compassion with a world that is running on empty. It is to let God love others through me and to be ready for this always, on all days, whether in the ditch or on the road. My job is to pour my life into the lives of others even in situations where there will be no one watching, no one applauding, no thanks given, no rewards received, no honoraria or travel expenses forthcoming, and no fruit to be seen, in places where the only joy is the inner certainty that I was in the right country at the right time, the right ditch by the right wayside. The joy will be in knowing that I do His will, which, you know, is quite enough to fill me.

Obeying Christ's call to pour out my life in compassion can still be a tricky thing. If I'm not careful, I can run low when I least expect it. For example, I'm finding it easier and easier these days to pour out myself overseas. I find myself reaching out easily to those who are so different from me. In fact, the hardest part of my job is making the adjustment back to easy street. The hardest part is keeping my focus on Him and on my daily duty when I leave those places where need is so apparent and return to a land where need is often hidden by affluence. The challenge is to love those who have everything just as much as I love those who have little or nothing.

The good news, of course, is that God's supply is just as dependable when I get home as it is when I am ministering abroad. And once I have the Holy Spirit in my life, though I may run low, there will always be more oil in my pot.

One day a few years back, I visited our son's church in Michigan's Upper Peninsula. I had the great joy of speaking to the friendly congregation in that small town. I spoke about the little pot of oil and shared many of the things I've spoken of in this book. Our eldest grandson, then just five years of age, doodled on his bulletin while I spoke. When the service was over, he showed me his drawing. He had been listening to the story as I told it and had portrayed it very well. Even then he was a good little artist. The widow was pouring out the oil into the jars while her sons watched. After finishing the picture, Danny had titled it: "The Little Pot of All."

I'll never know whether it was his Nana's English accent or divine inspiration that made him hear *all* instead of *oil*. But I do know he hit the meaning on the head. When you are poured out, the Holy Spirit has only just begun His work in you. He will pour in all you need on a moment-by-moment basis—and day by day and hour by hour. If you're feeling empty, depleted, or out of steam, if you're waiting for the wind, first cry to Him for help. Then start pouring and feel the goodness start to flow.

All my ransomed powers and all the things I own,
All my life's ambitions I lay down at Your throne.
All my love and laughter and all the pain and tears,
All my apprehension and all my doubts and fears.

All my awful failures and all my gains and loss,
All my small shortcomings I lay down at Your cross.
All my lies and boasting and all my sin and pride,
All the guile I practice and all the hate I hide.

Give all the grace I plead for, and all forgiveness brings.
Send all the peace I long for until my spirit sings,

Till all the tears forgotten and sins I can't recall,
Till Jesus, all is Jesus, and He is all in all!

Fill all my empty spaces,
heal all the hurts I've borne.
Give me the power to change my life;
I need to be reborn.
So take my life, Lord Jesus;
know all my days I'll spend
Investing in Your kingdom work
till life itself shall end.

Send all the power I ask for; give all the grace and peace,
All Your present presence, the Spirit's sweet release.
Give all Your grand dynamic You want me to impart,
All this sweet enabling, please pour into my heart.

Jill Briscoe

PRESSURE PROOF YOUR MARRIAGE
Family First Series, #3
DENNIS & BARBARA RAINEY ISBN 978-1-59052-211-0

Dennis and Barbara Rainey show you how to use pressure to your benefit, building intimacy with each other and with the Lord.

TWO HEARTS PRAYING AS ONE
Family First Series, #2
DENNIS & BARBARA RAINEY ISBN 978-1-59052-035-2

Praying together daily is the best thing you can do for your marriage. Start right away with Dennis and Barbara Rainey's interactive guide!

GROWING A SPIRITUALLY STRONG FAMILY
Family First Series, #1
DENNIS & BARBARA RAINEY ISBN 978-1-57673-778-1

Down-to-earth advice, encouraging stories, timely insights, and life-changing truths from FamilyLife's Dennis and Barbara Rainey direct parents on the path to leaving a godly family legacy.

WRESTLING WITH GOD
Prayer That Never Gives Up
GREG LAURIE ISBN 978-1-59052-044-4

You struggle with God in your own unique way. See how your struggle can result in the most rewarding relationship with Him!

SMALL BOOKS
BIG CHANGE

BIG CHANGE

How Good Is Good Enough?
Andy Stanley ISBN 978-1-59052-274-5
(Available October 2003)

Find out why Jesus taught that goodness is not even a requirement to enter heaven—and why Christianity is beyond fair.

A Little Pot of Oil
Jill Briscoe ISBN 978-1-59052-234-9
(Available October 2003)

What if He's asking you to pour out more than you can give? Step into the forward motion of God's love—and find the power of the Holy Spirit!

In the Secret Place
For God and You Alone
J. Otis Ledbetter ISBN 978-1-57673-252-3
(Available September 2003)

Receive answers to some of life's most perplexing questions— and find deeper fellowship alone in the place where God dwells.

The Air I Breathe
Worship as a Way of Life
Louie Giglio ISBN 978-1-59052-153-3

When we are awakened to the wonder of God's character and the cross of Christ, all of life becomes worship unto God.

SMALL BOOKS
BIG CHANGE

BIG CHANGE

OUR JEALOUS GOD
Love That Won't Let Me Go
BILL GOTHARD ISBN 978-1-59052-225-7
(Available October 2003)

God's intense jealousy for you is your highest honor, an overflowing of sheer grace. And when you understand it better, it becomes a pathway to countless blessings.

THE POWER OF CRYING OUT
When Prayer Becomes Mighty
BILL GOTHARD ISBN 978-1-59052-037-6

Bill Gothard explains how a crisis that is humanly impossible is an opportunity for God to show His power—the moment you cry out to Him.

THE FIRE THAT IGNITES
Living in the Power of the Holy Spirit
TONY EVANS ISBN 978-1-59052-083-3

Tony Evans reveals how the Holy Spirit can ignite a fire in your life today, transforming you from a sleepwalker into a wide-awake witness for Him!

GOD IS UP TO SOMETHING GREAT
Turning Your Yesterdays into Better Tomorrows
TONY EVANS ISBN 978-1-59052-038-3

Are you living with regrets? Discover the positives of your past. Tony Evans shows how God intends to use your experiences—good, bad, and ugly—to lead you toward His purpose for your life.

SMALL BOOKS
BIG CHANGE

BIG CHANGE

SMALL BOOKS
BIG CHANGE

Printed in the United States
by Baker & Taylor Publisher Services